Alphabets & Numbers FOR KIDS

Nora Artchan

THIS BOOK BELONGS TO

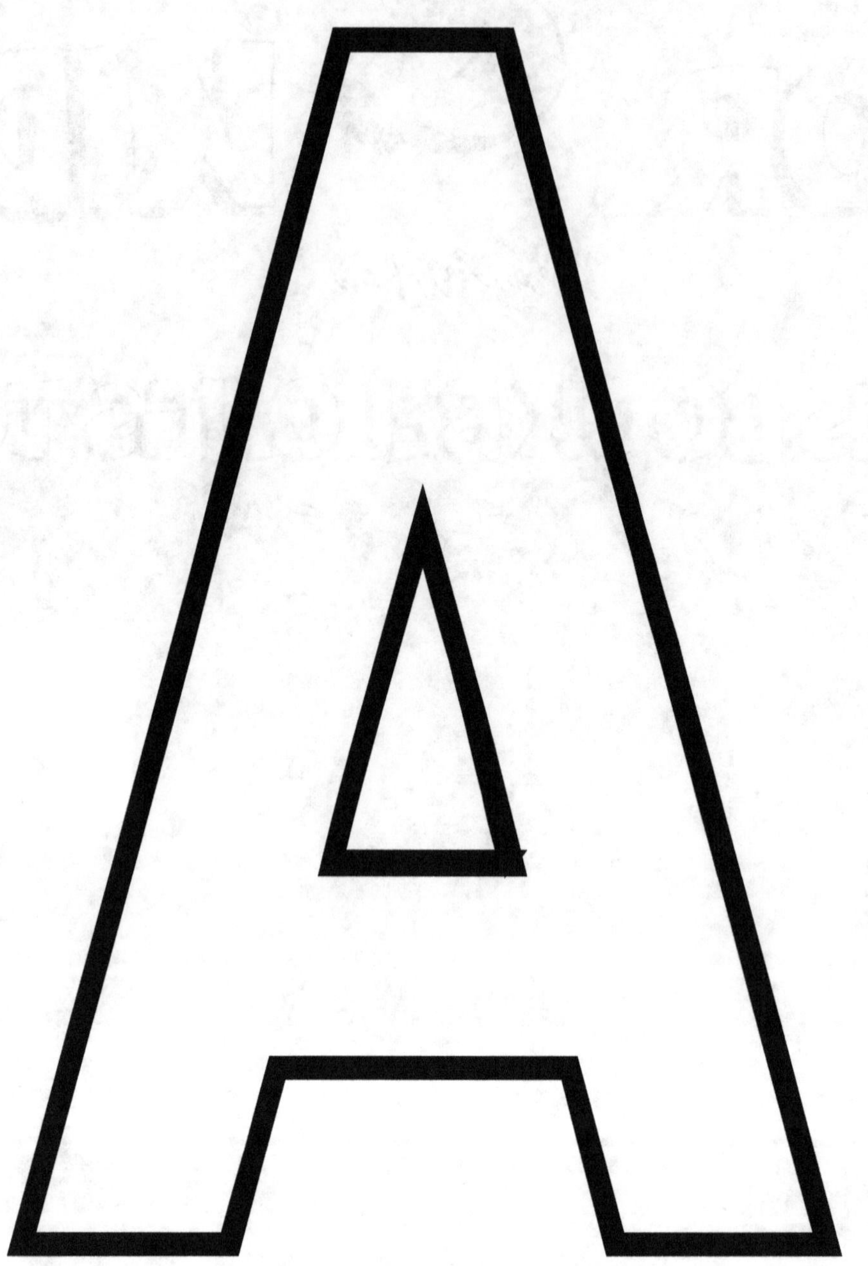

AIRPLANE

BOAT

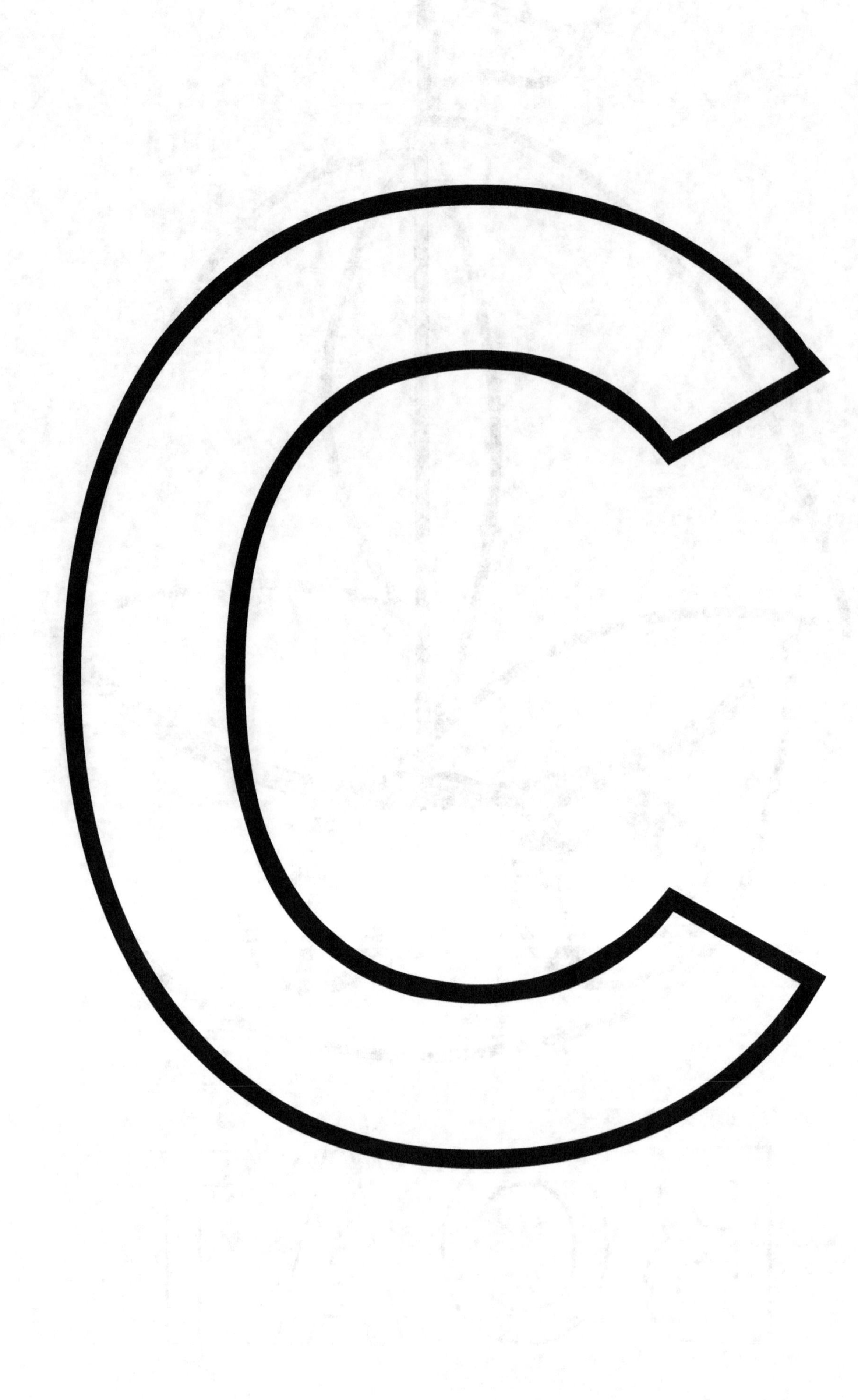

CACTUS

DOG

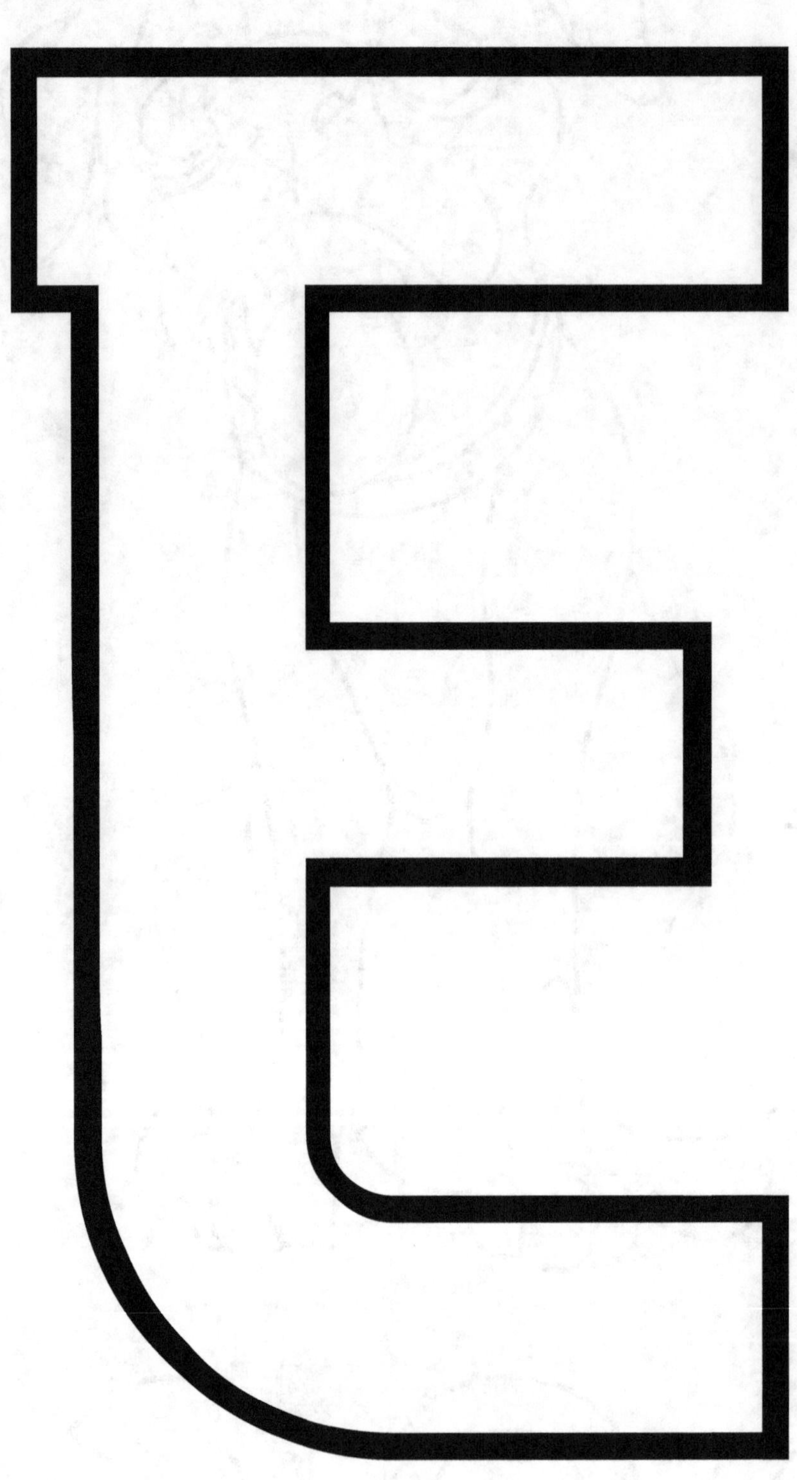

ELEPHANT

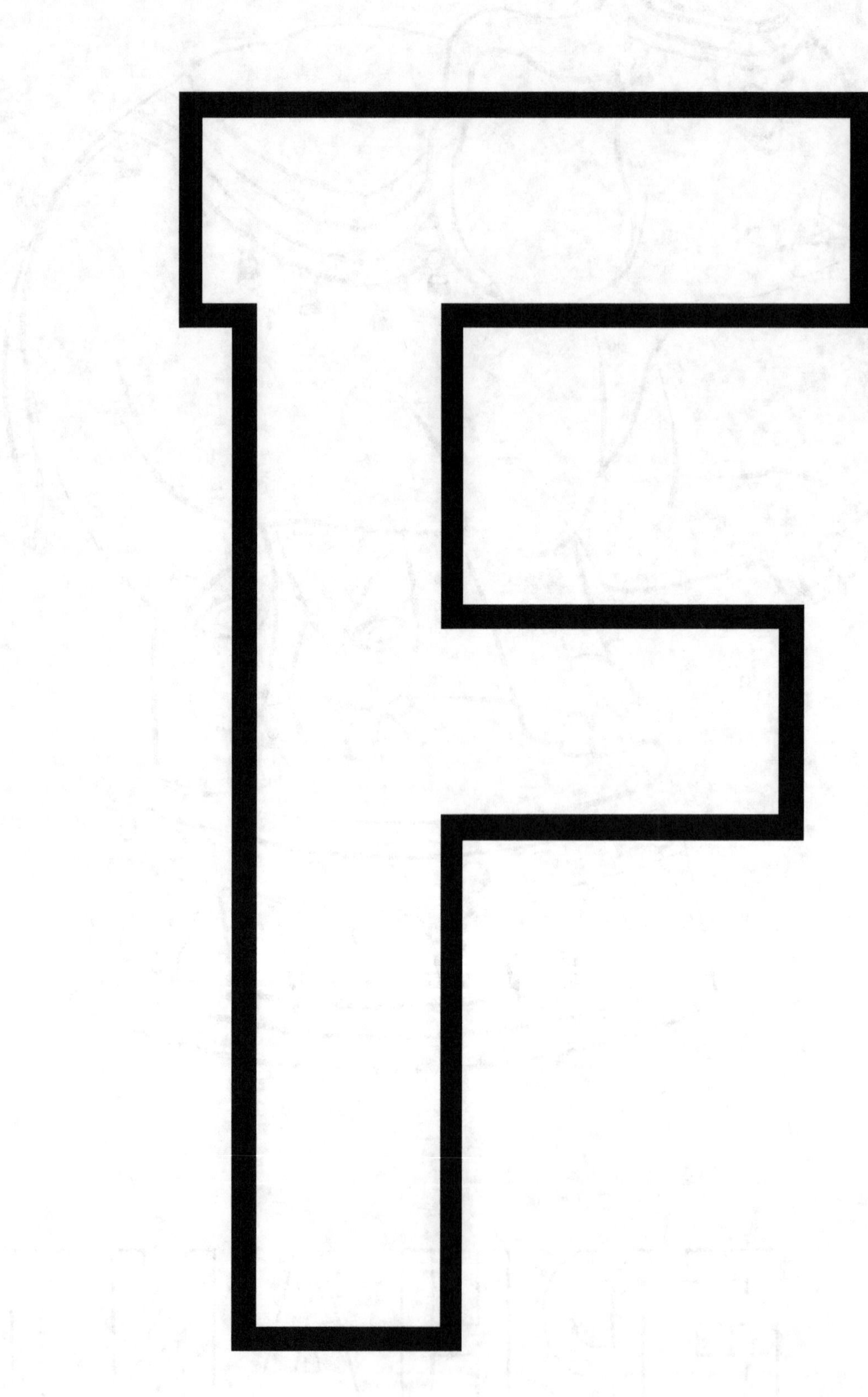

FROG

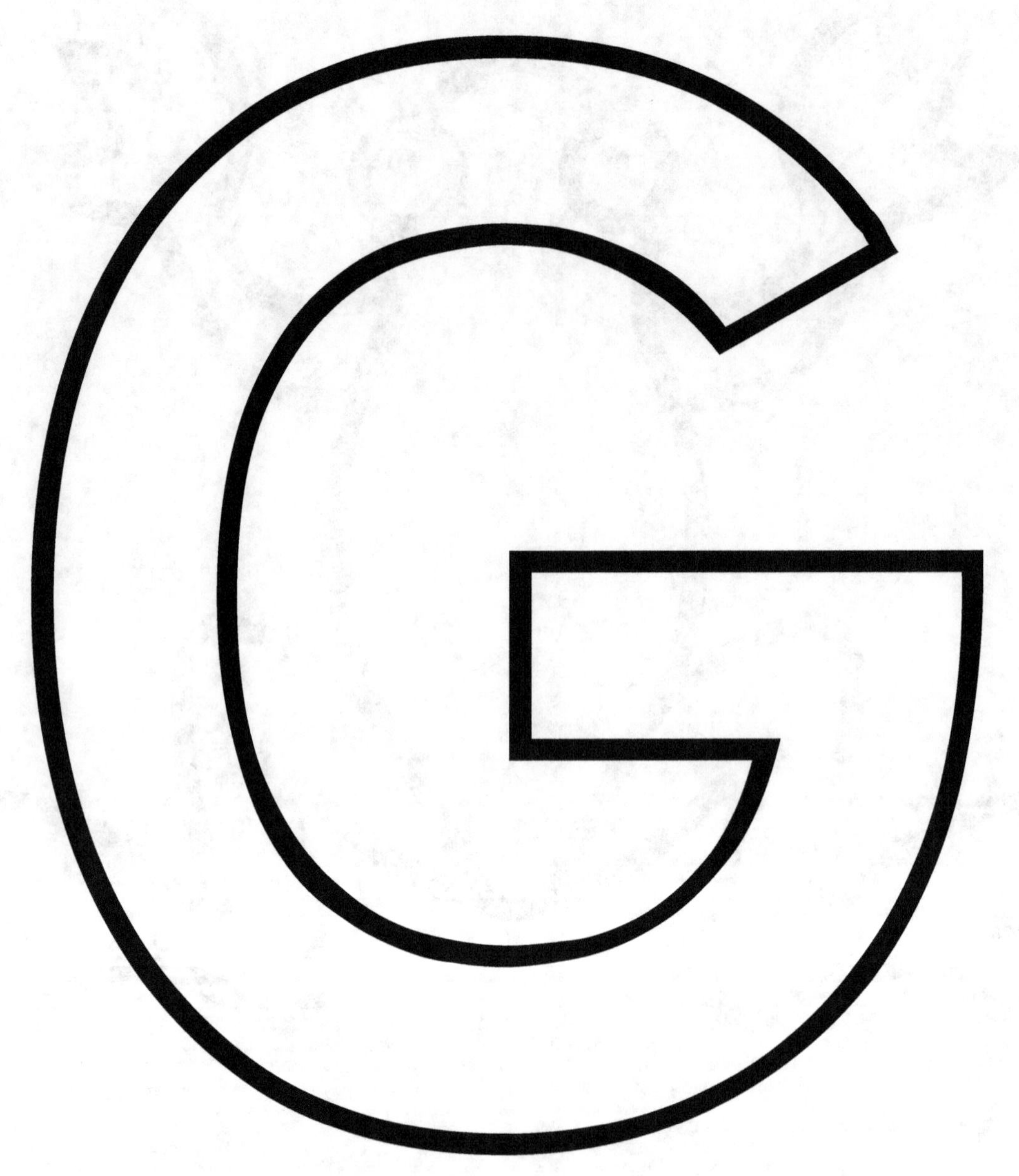

GIRAFFE

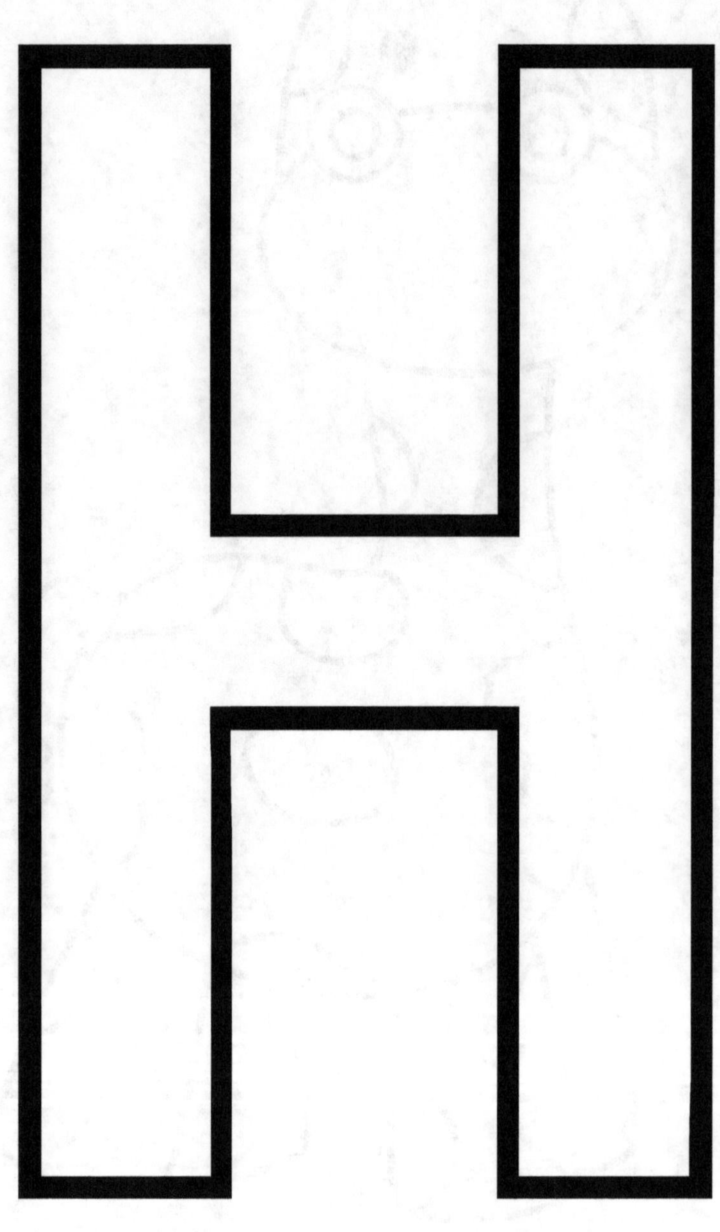

HORSE

IGUANA

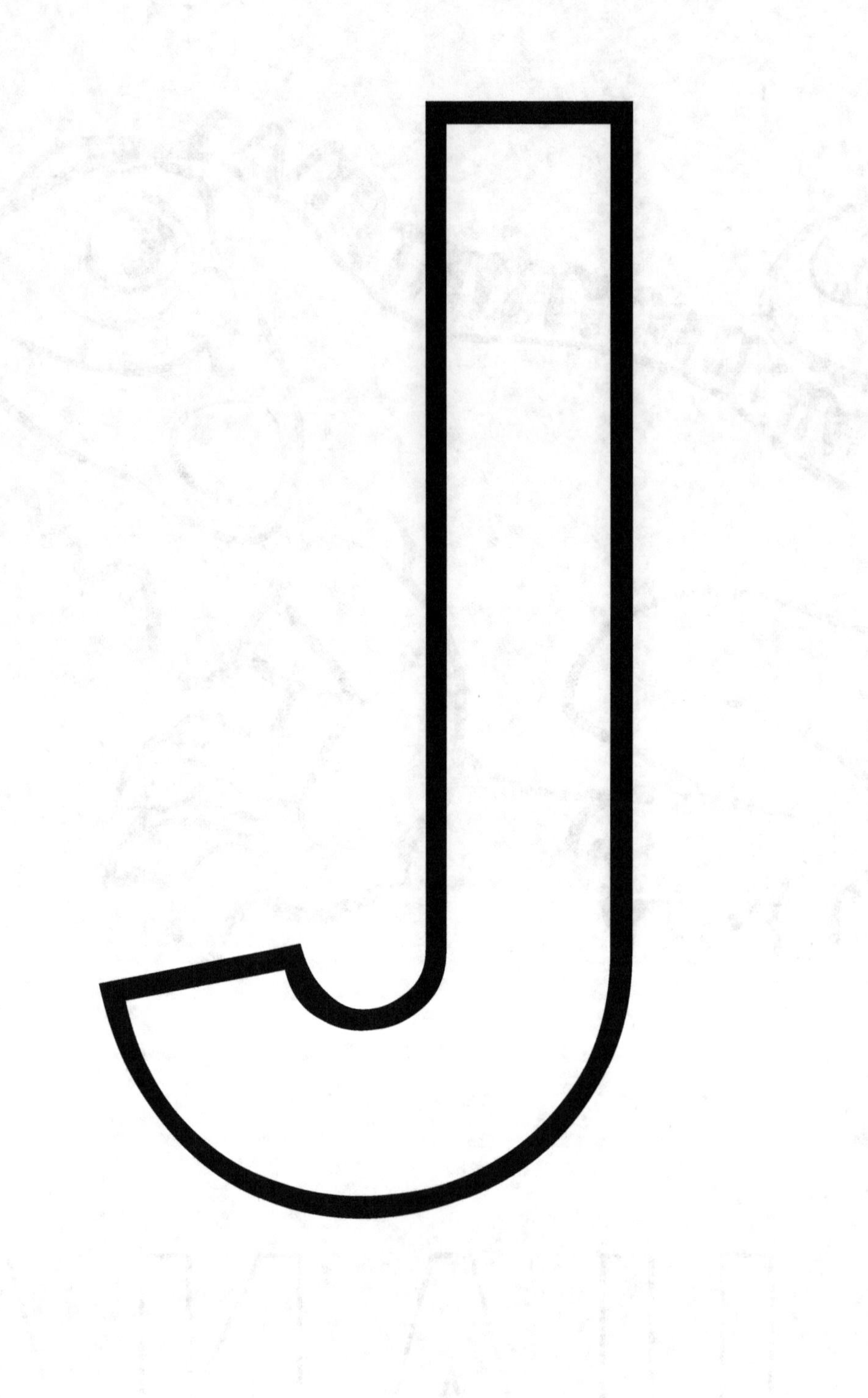

JELLYFISH

K

KANGAROO

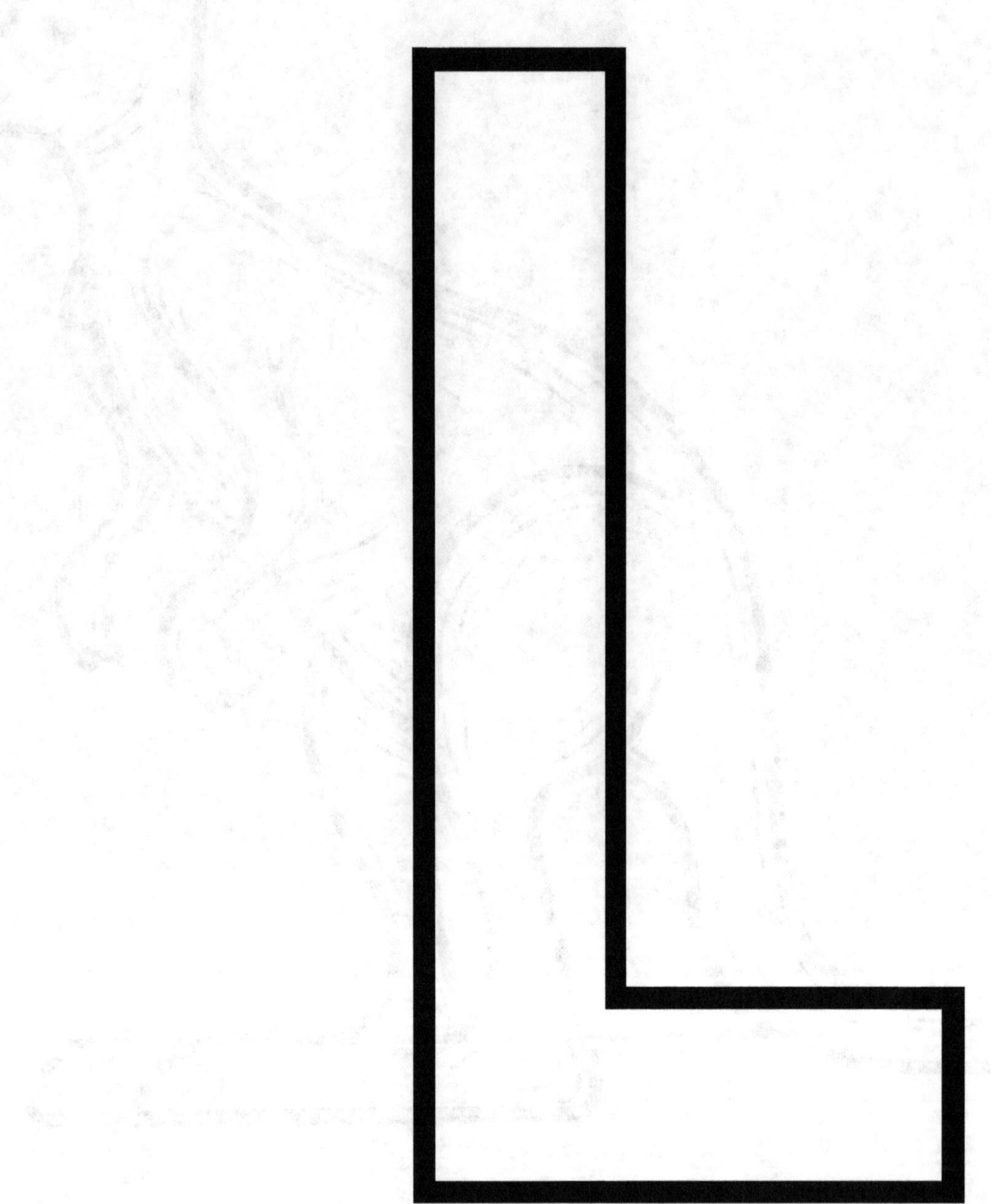

LION

M

MONKEY

NEWT

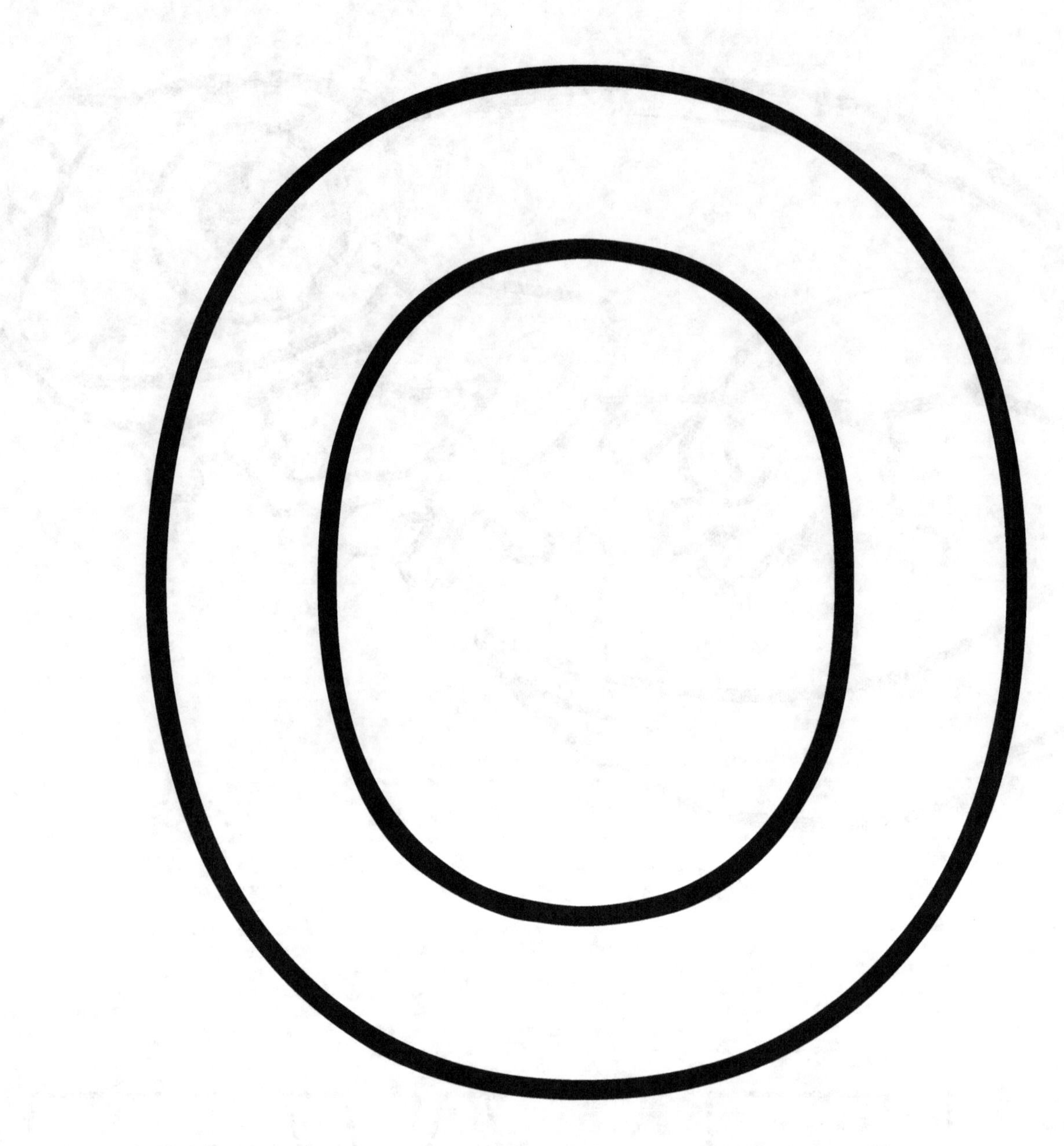

OCTOPUS

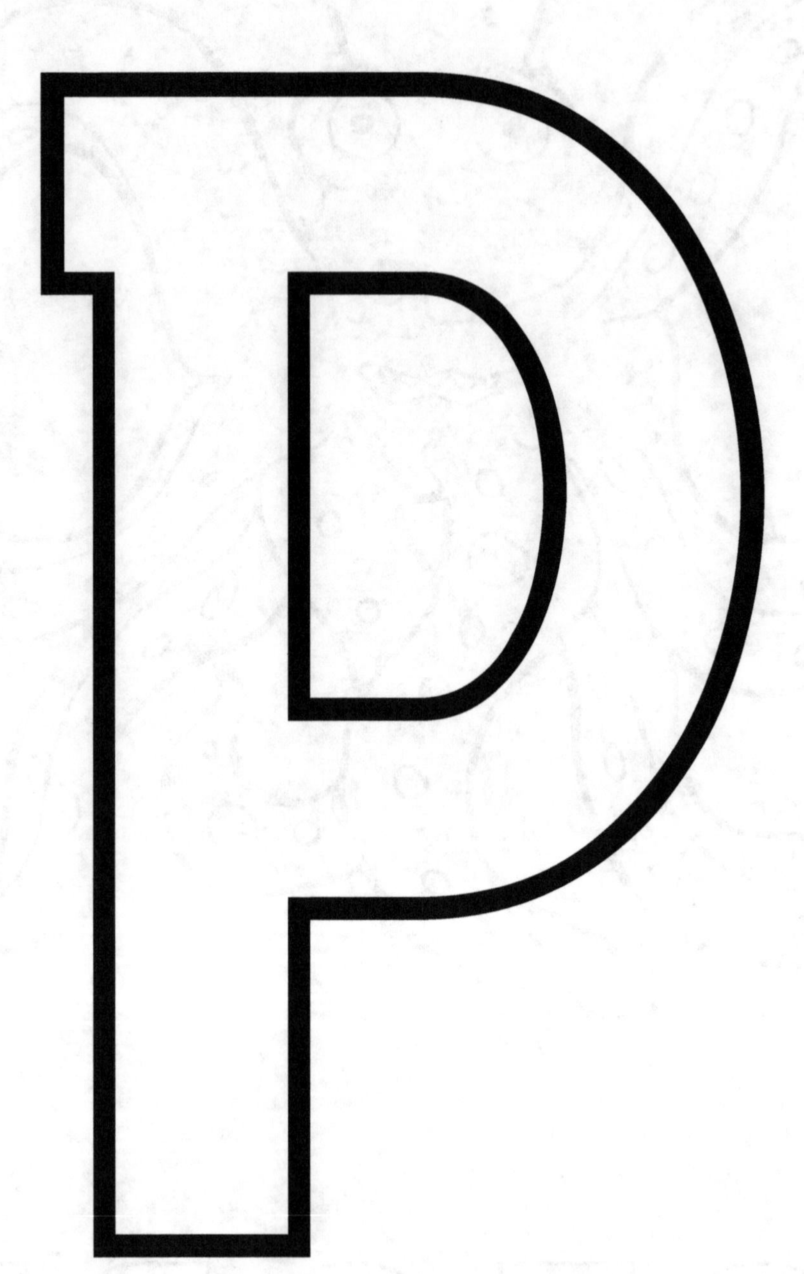

PANDA

QUEEN

RABBIT

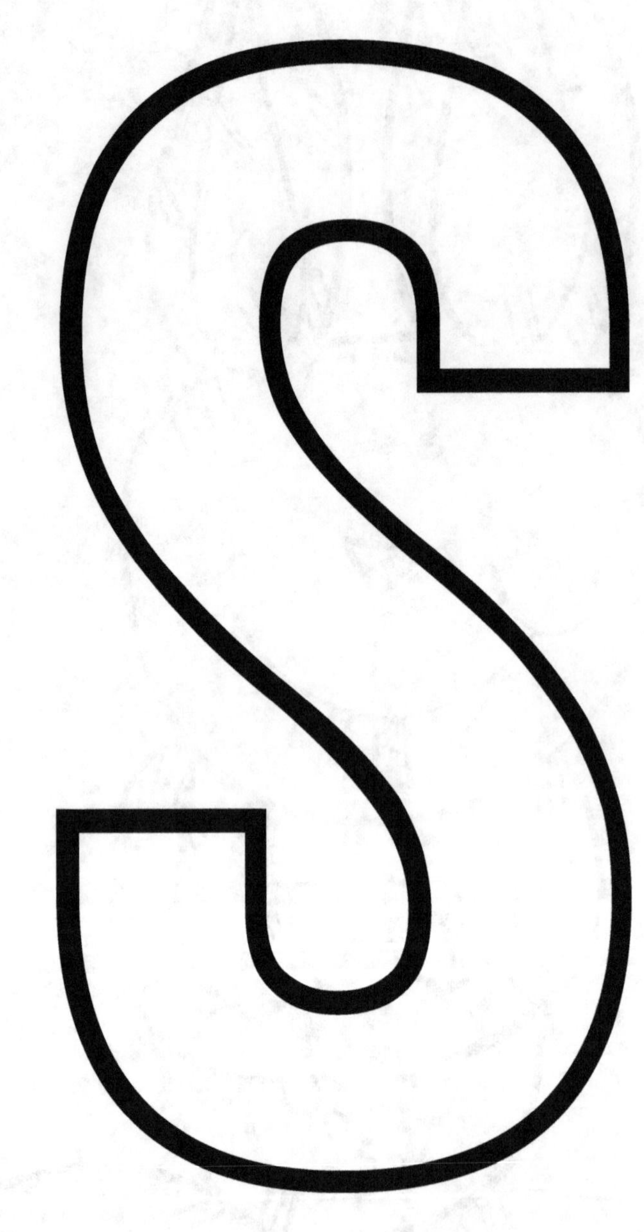

SNAKE

TURTLE

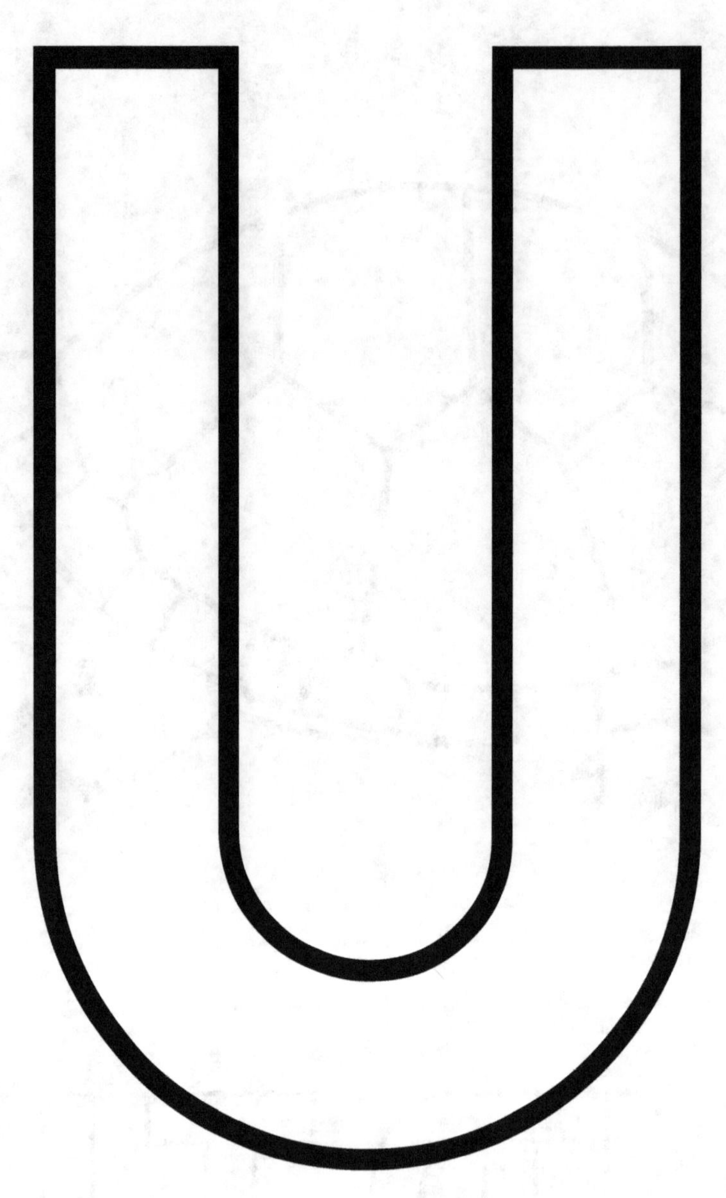

UNICORN

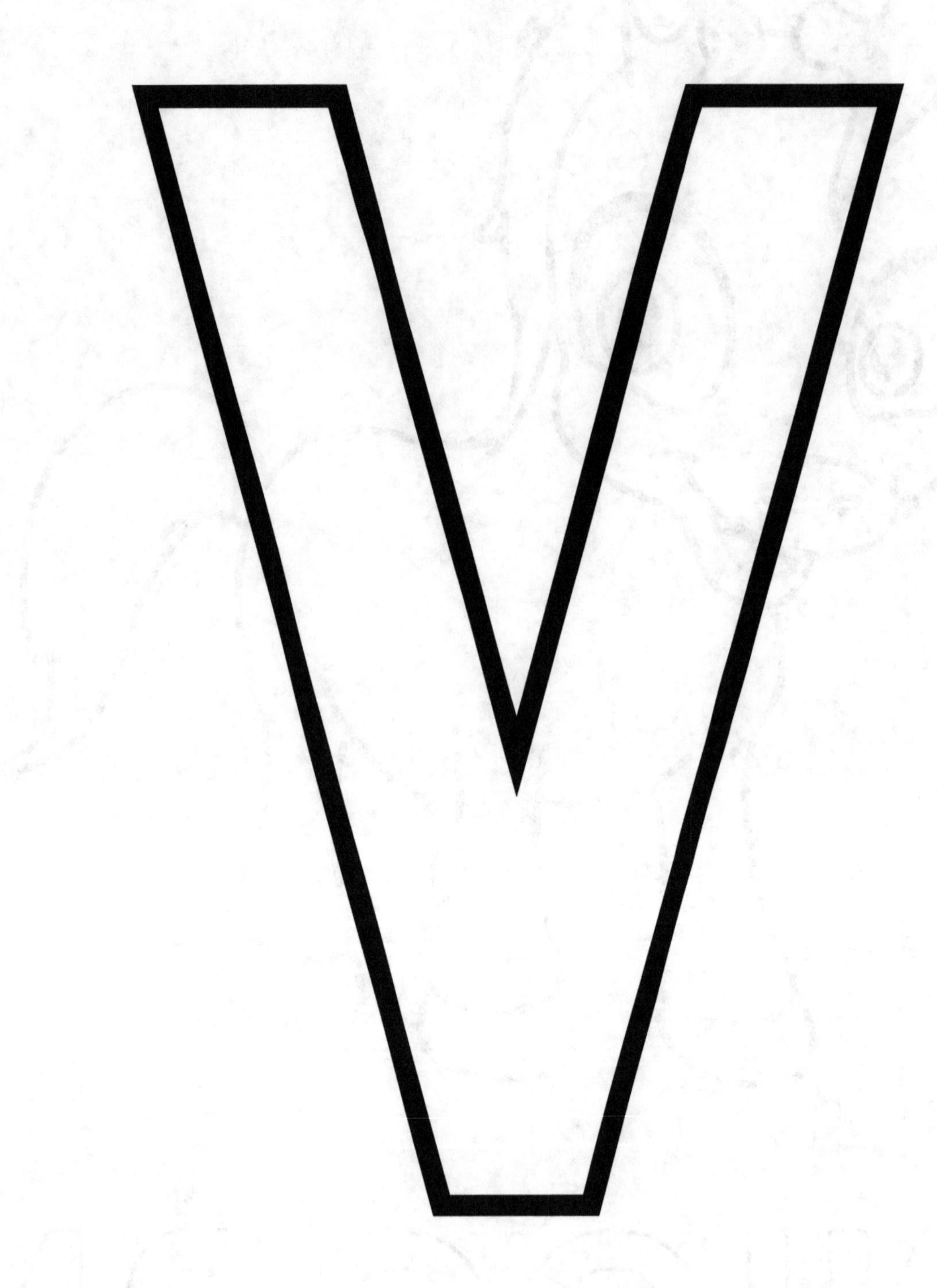

VOILIN

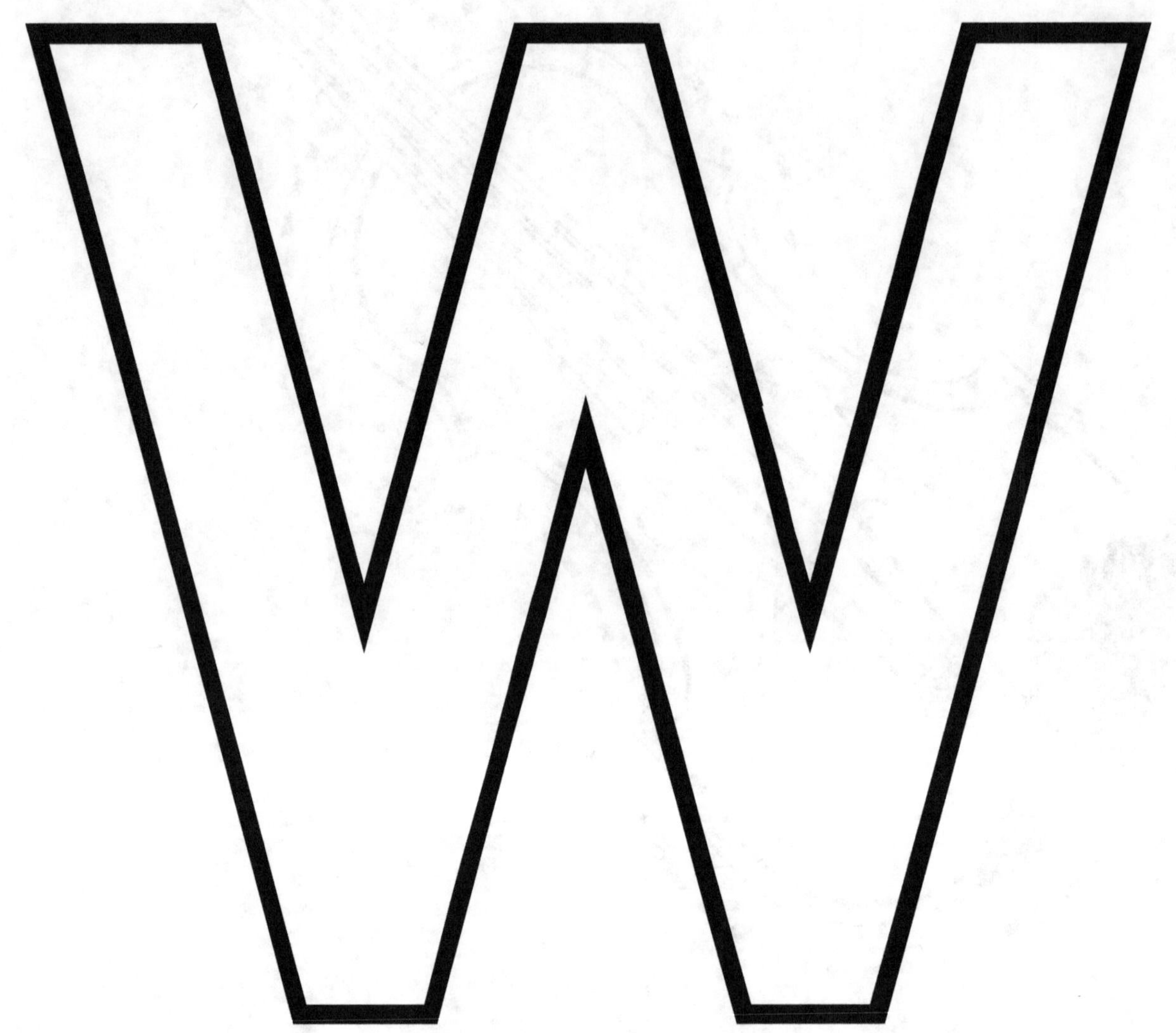

WATERMELON

X

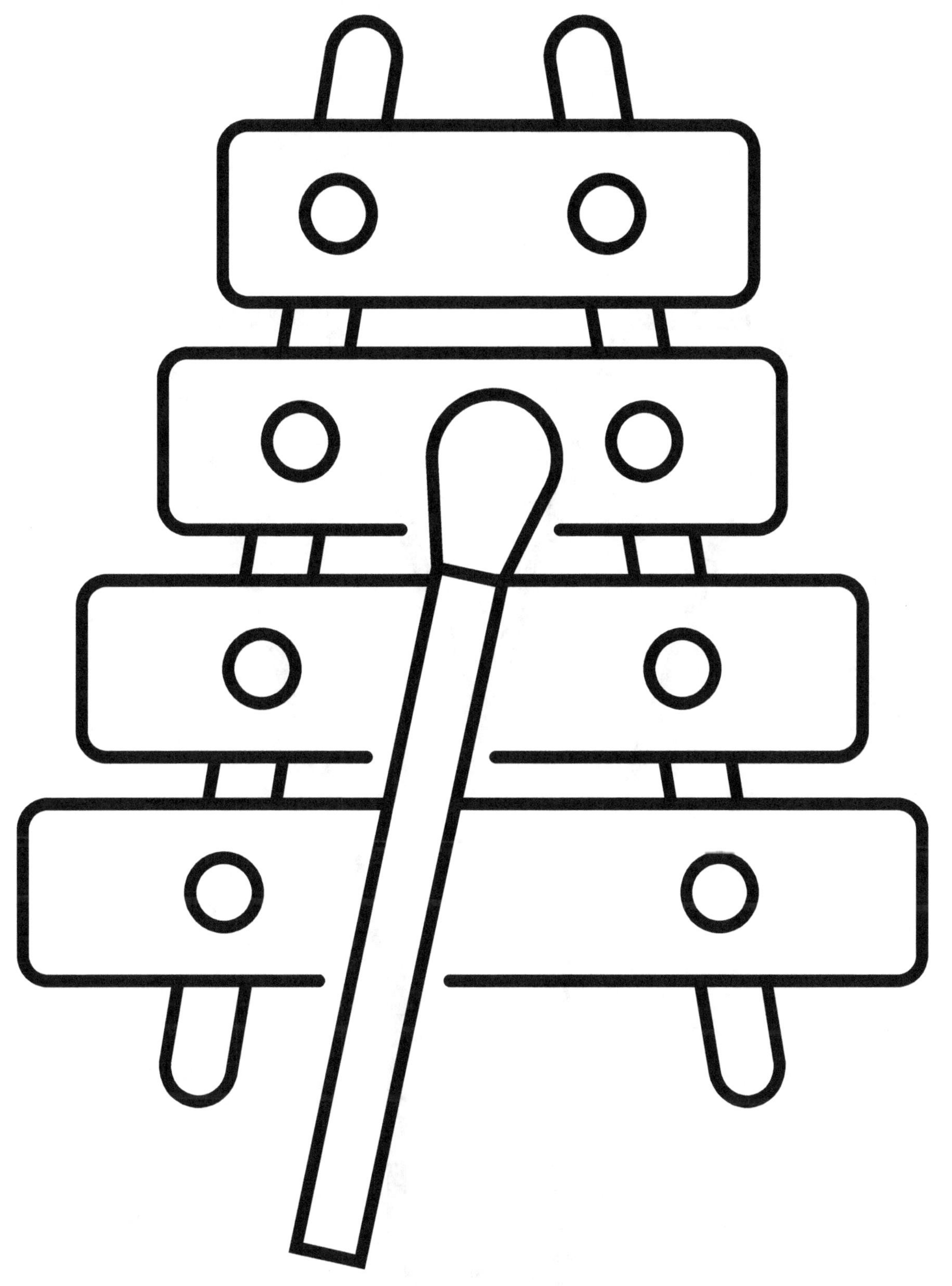

XYLOPHONE

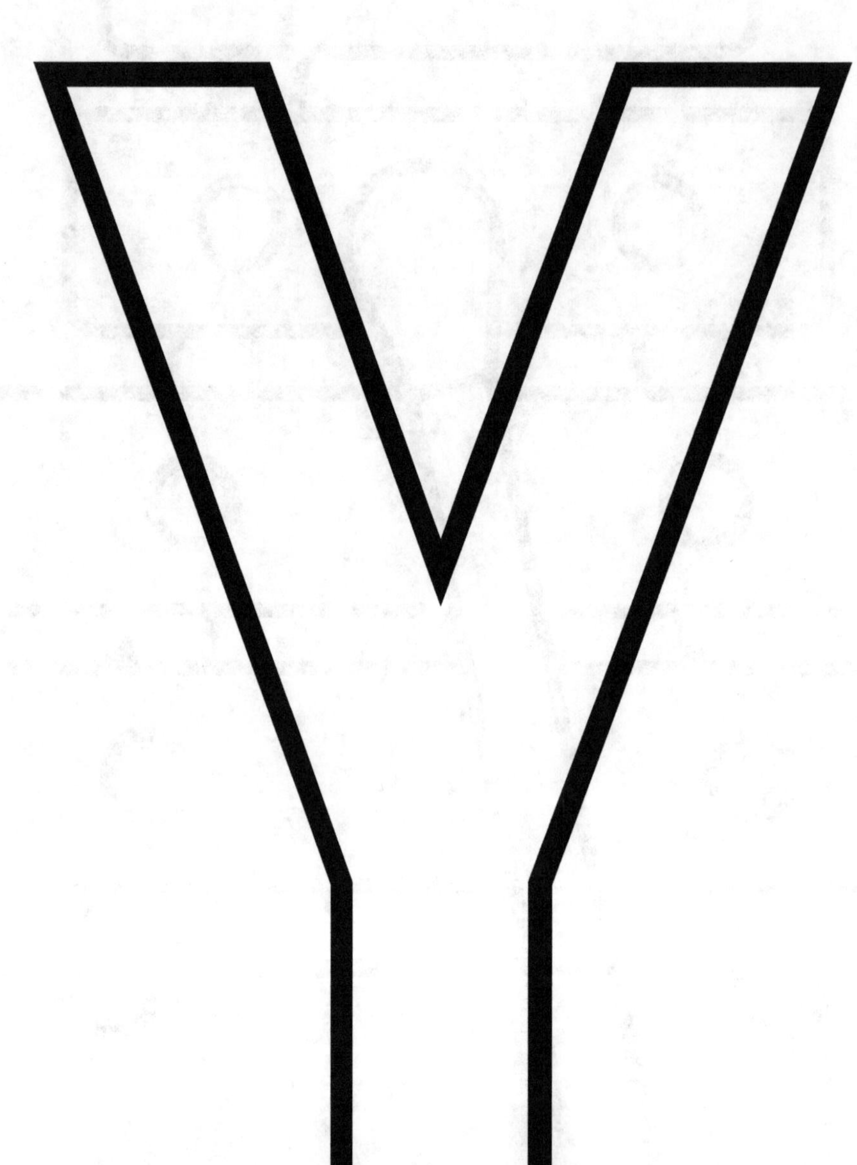

YAK

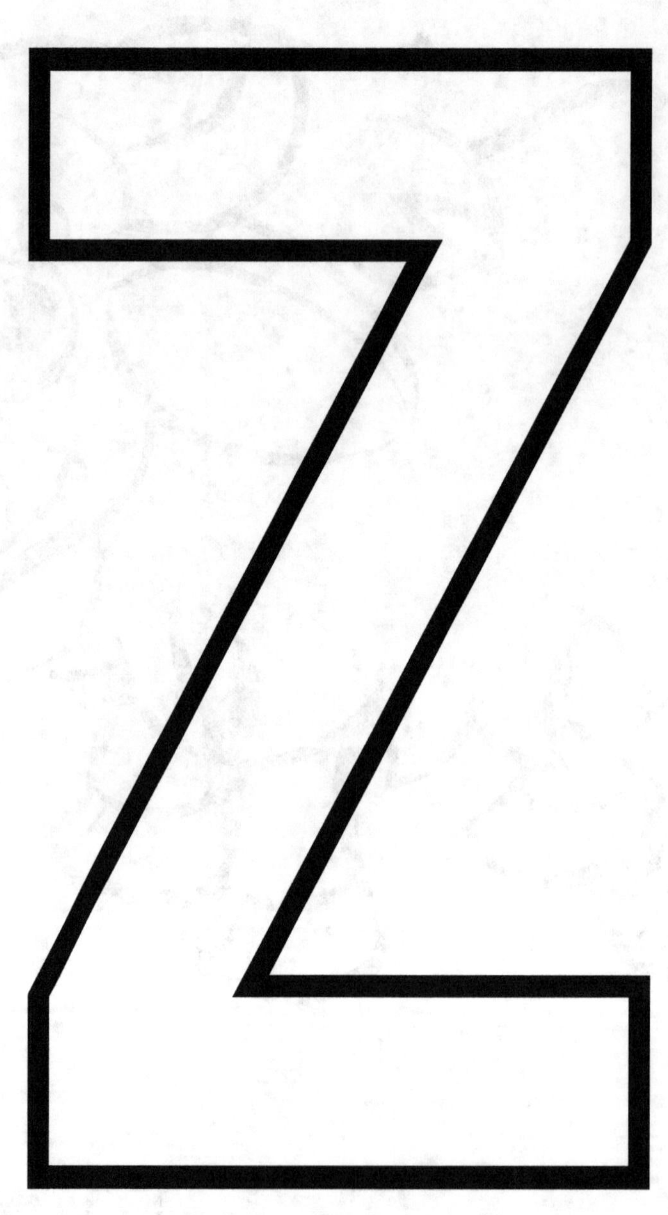

ZEBRA

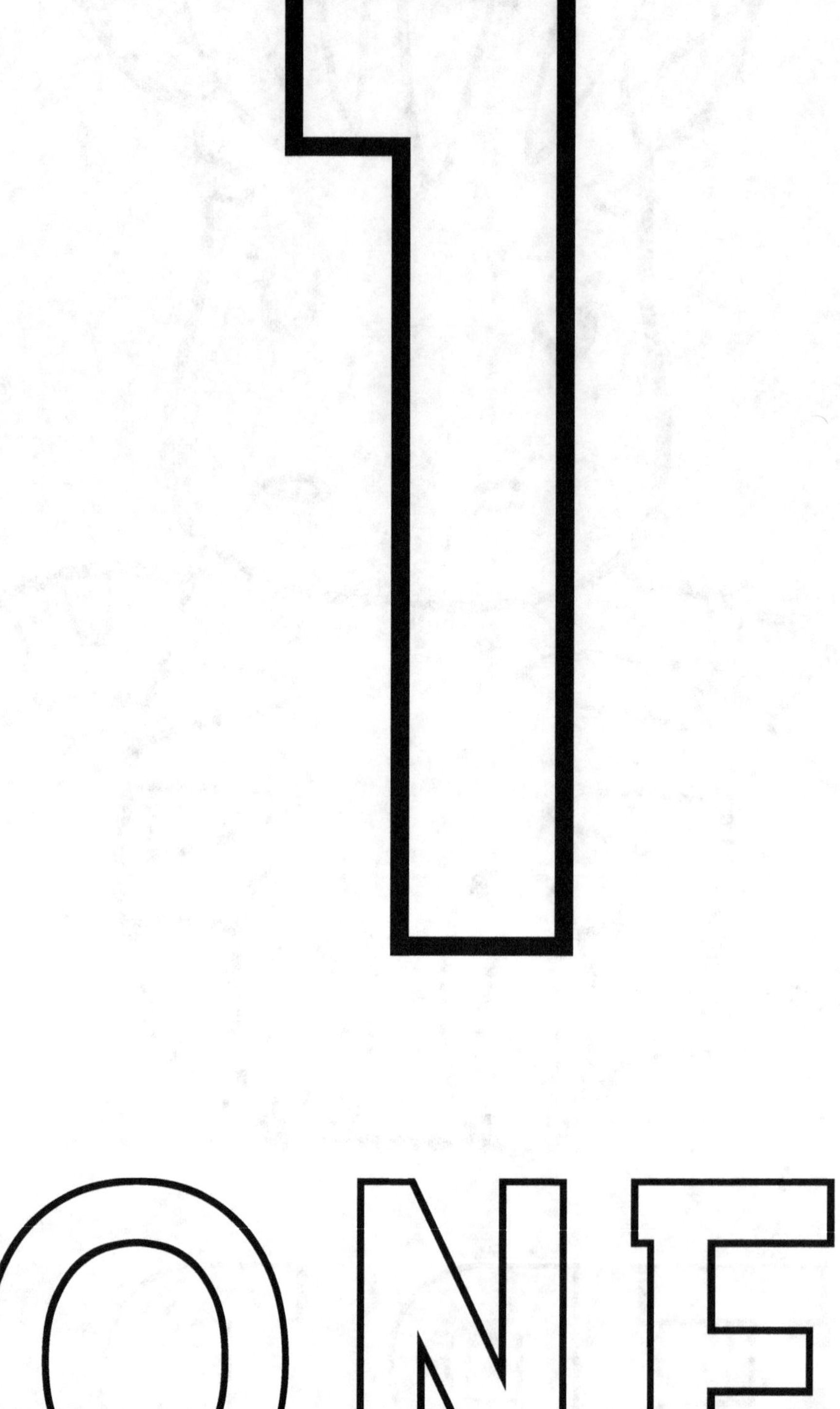

1
ONE

2

TWO

3

THREE

4
FOUR

5
FIVE

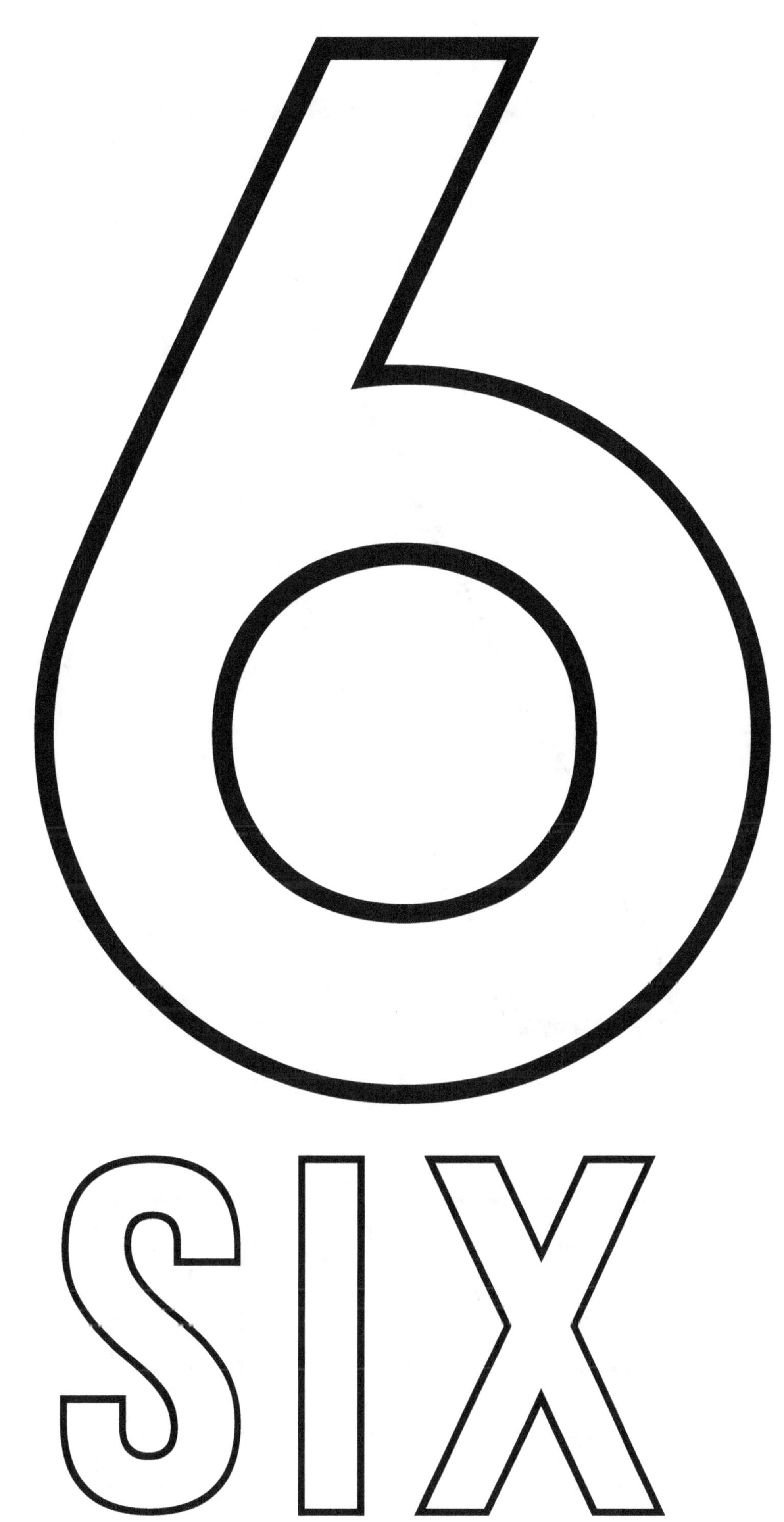

6
SIX

7

SEVEN

8
EIGHT

9
NINE

10

TEN

11

ELEVEN

12

TWELVE

13

THIRTEEN

14

FOURTEEN

15

FIFTEEN

16

SIXTEEN

17

SEVENTEEN

18

EIGHTEEN

19

NINETEEN

20

TWENTY

ONE CAT

TWO DOGS

THREE BIRDS

FOUR UNICORNS

FIVE TURTLES

SIX CATERPILLARS

SEVEN RABBITS

EIGHT CLOCKS

NINE SNAKES

TEN CARS

ELEVEN TRUCKS

TWELVE APPLES

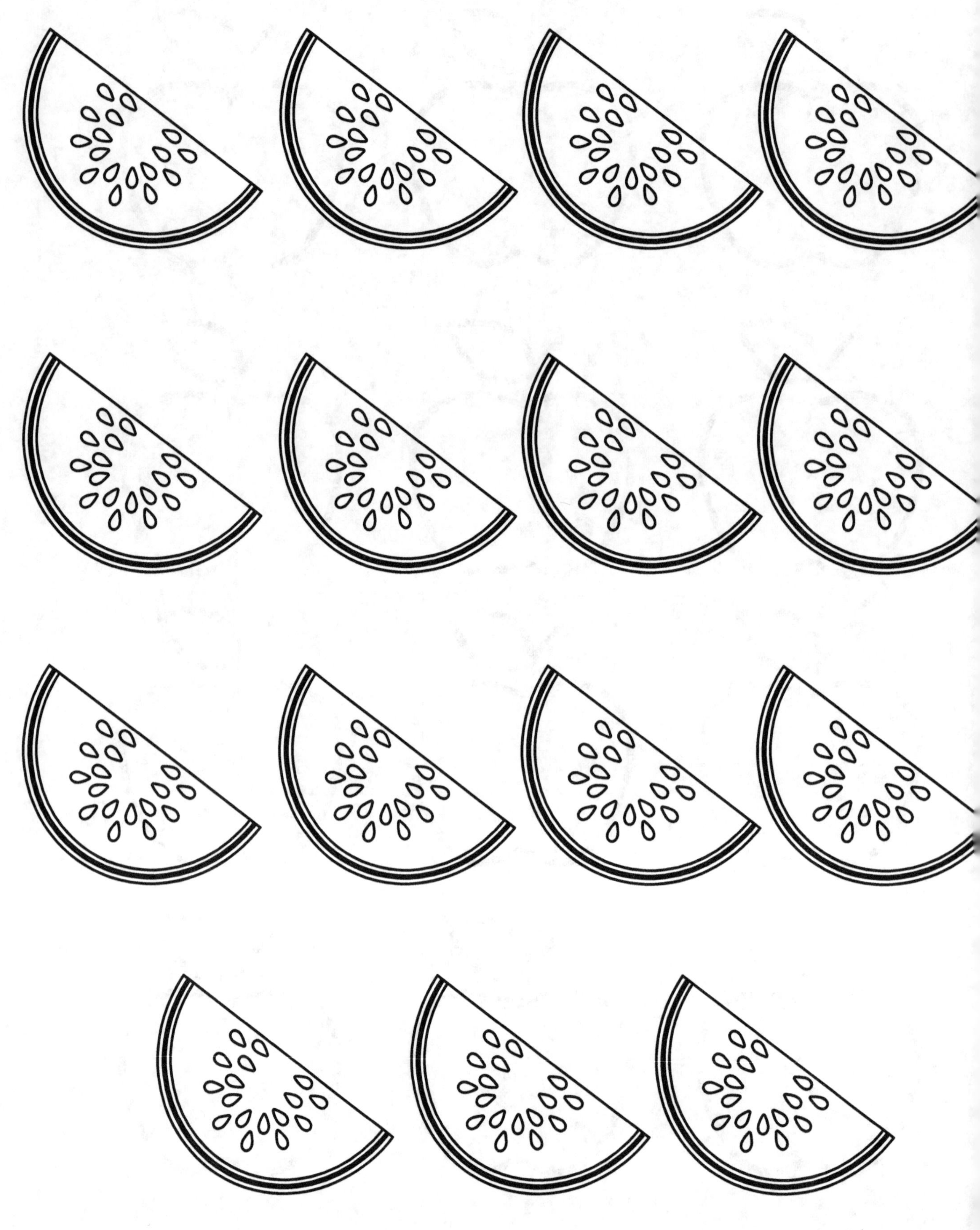

THIRTEEN WATERMELONS

FOURTEEN FLOWERS

FIFTEEN CRABS

SIXTEEN BALLS

SEVENTEEN BOOKS

EIGHTEEN
CARROTS

NINETEEN TOMATOES

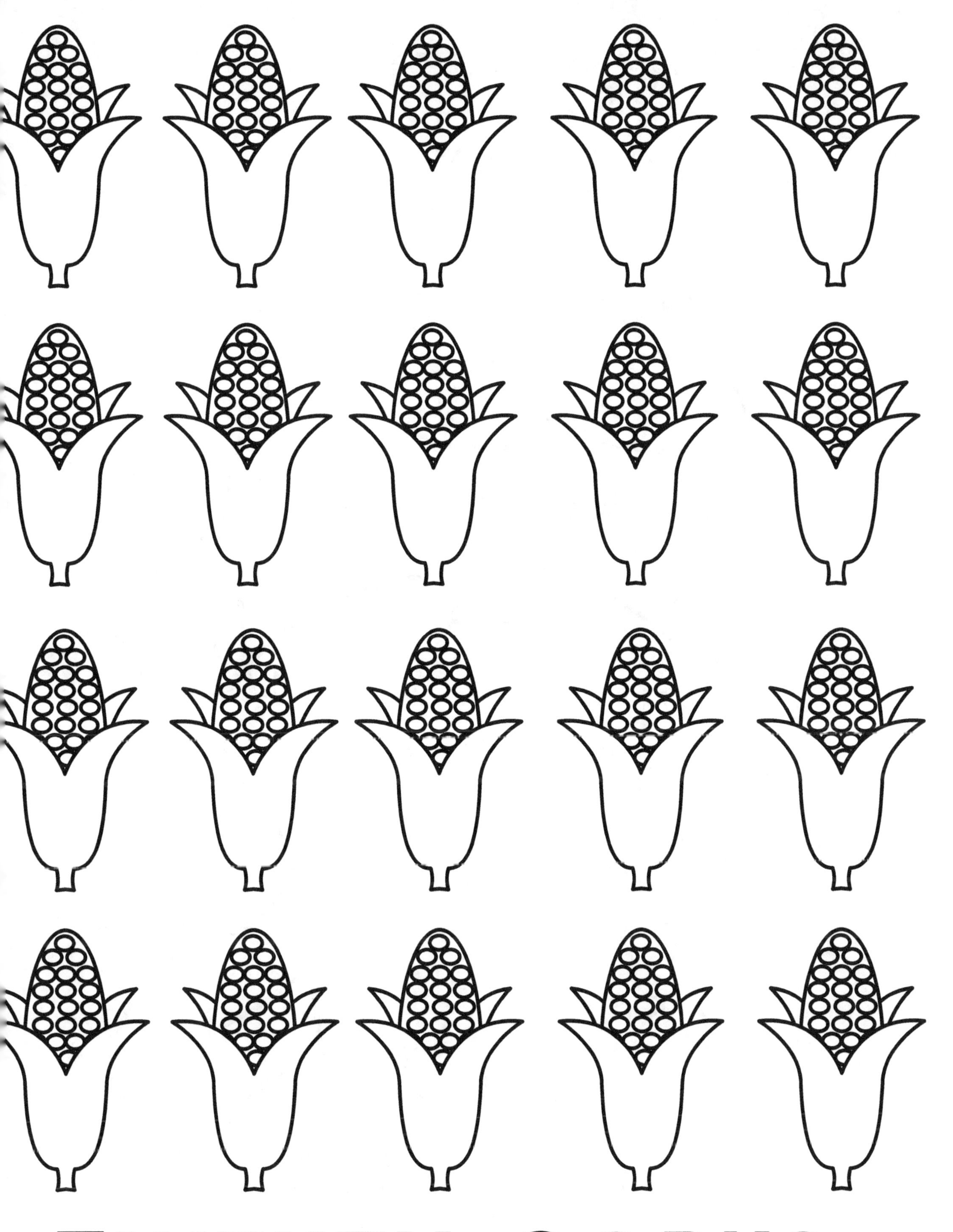
TWENTY CORNS

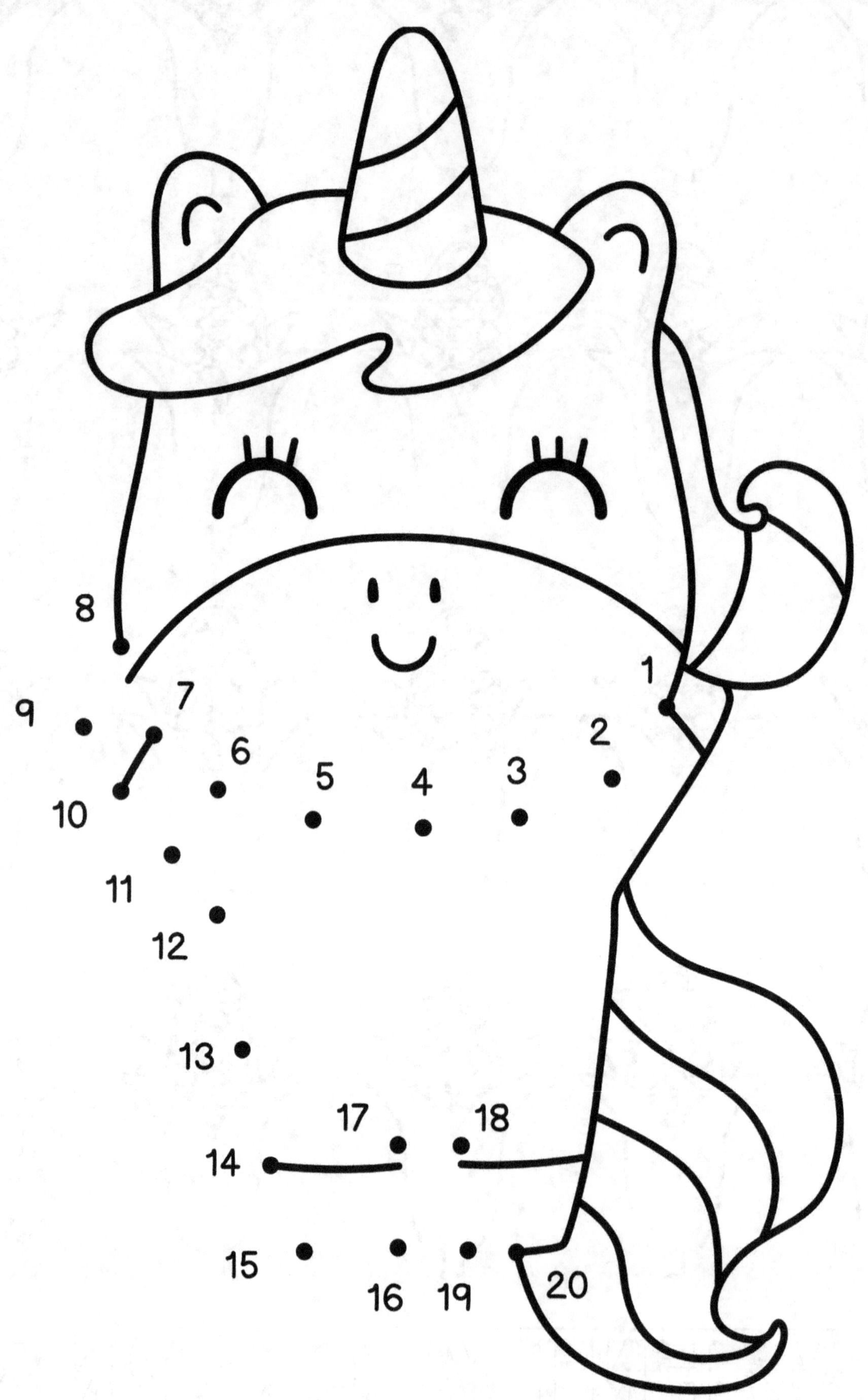

8
9
7
1
10
6
5
4
3
2
11
12
13
17
18
14
15
16
19
20

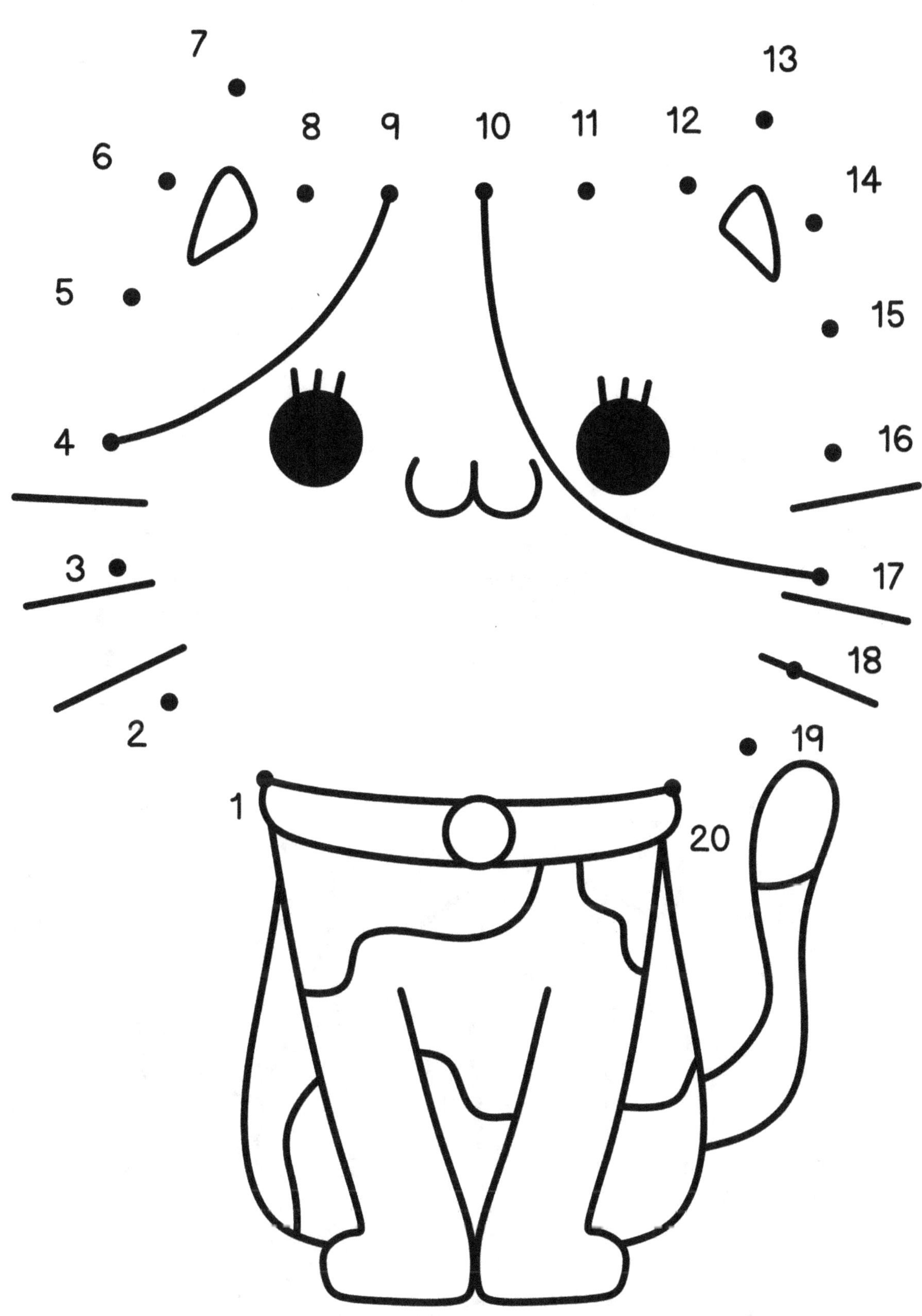

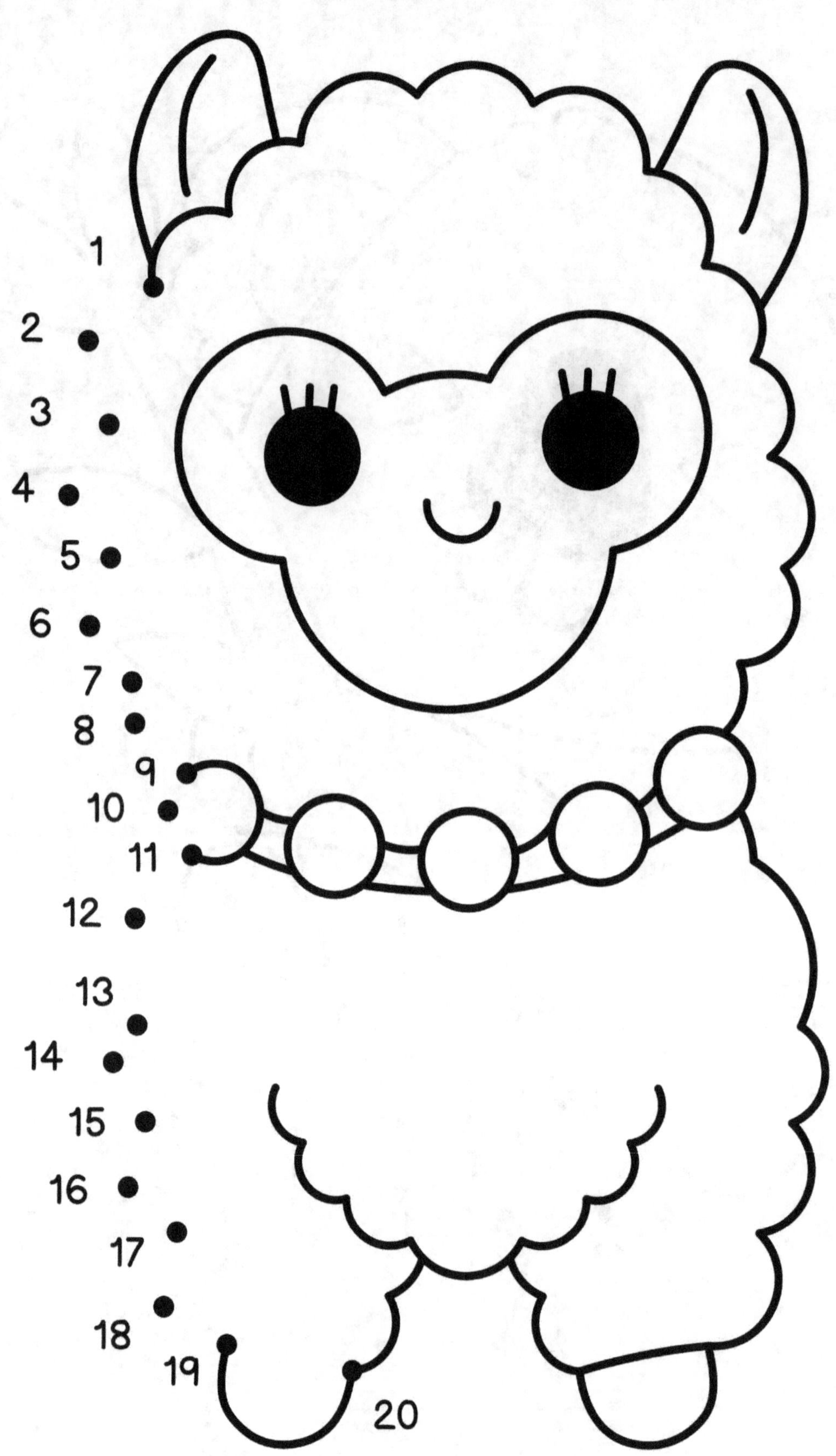

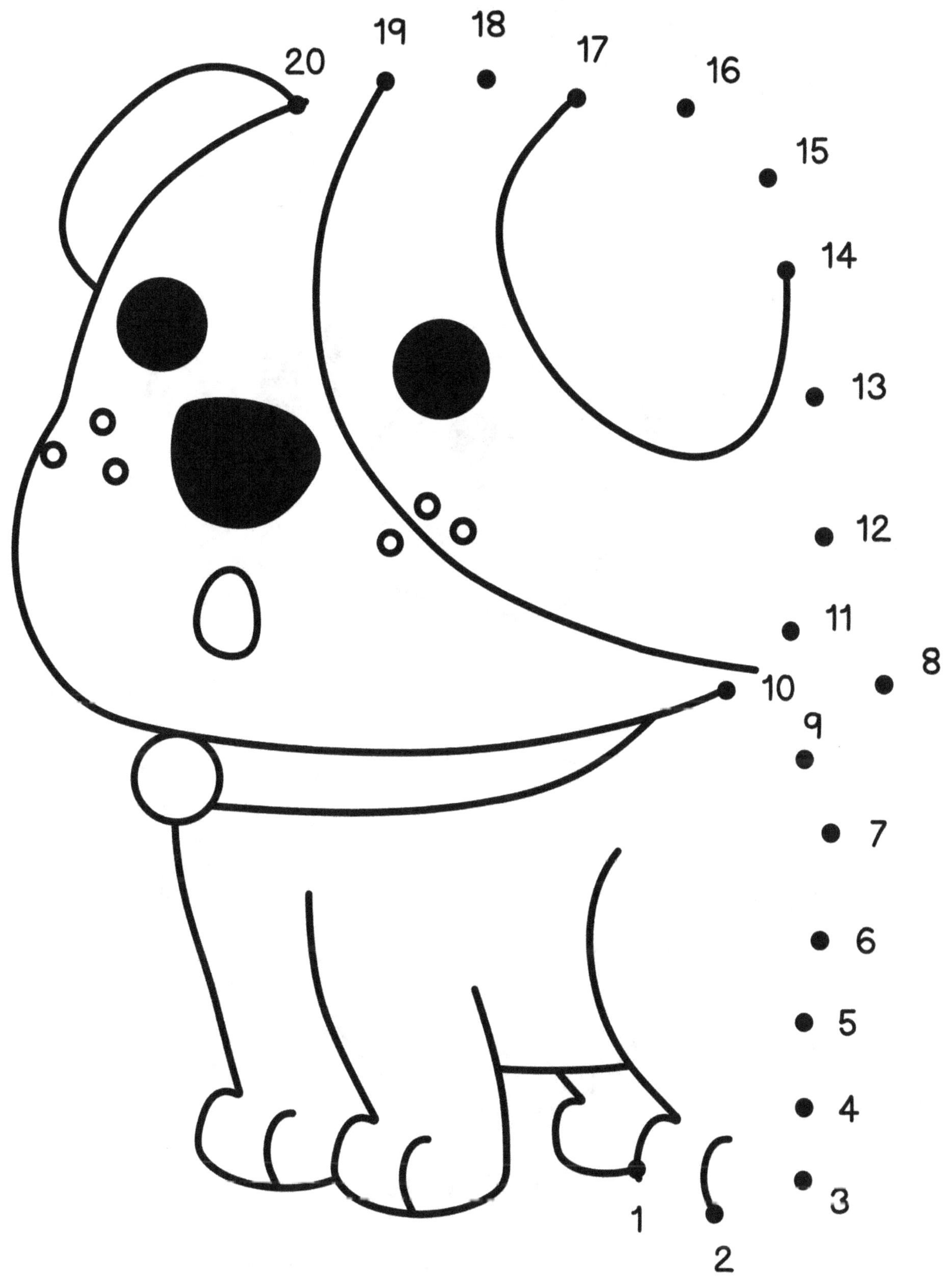